**Dedicated to
Paul, Matt & Charlie**

This book belongs to:

_____

Hello there, Super Star

I am so excited to see how you get on with your new book
and all the new things you learn and achieve…

Maybe you can teach your friends and family some things too.

Take a page each day and enjoy the things that have been set out
for you.

If you can't do something some day because of the weather
or you don't have something or whatever,
that's OK, you can do it again another day.

If you really like doing something you have done
on a different day, then feel free to repeat that game, task,
exercise again on another day after you have
completed your current page.

Most importantly of all…

Enjoy!

What to do...

Complete just 1 page each day

Every day you need to write the date

Record how you feel by circling or colouring a face

Really Happy   Happy   OK   Sad   Really Sad or Angry

Complete the questions/tasks each day

There is always a fun puzzle/picture for you to do each day

If there is something you don't understand ask someone older to help you.

Say your affirmations every day and believe them e.g. "I am clever."

Feelings

S C L E H A P P Y C
P L O L X Z S Y T A
E W V N L C V K F M
C N E P T H I G F U
I J D L L E Z T W S
A G O X K E N Q E E
L L O Y Z R A T C D
F A O C F F N S S U
U D H K C U K R E N
Q E U E N L L K D D

Cheerful   Excited   Content   Pleased
Special   Joyful   Happy   Amused
            Glad   Loved

Day 1

Date: _____

Today, I feel…

Today, I am so happy and grateful for:

1. _____

2. _____

3. _____

Something I don't enjoy doing very much (e.g. washing the dishes)	How can I make it more enjoyable to do? (e.g. sing along to the radio)

Tick what you have done today:

○ Made my bed
○ Brushed my teeth
○ Told someone I loved them
○ Gave someone a hug
○ Smiled
○ Helped someone at home
○ Did a chore without being asked

**Repeat 3 times:
I am good**

Draw a picture of something that makes you smile!

Colour the Picture!

Day 2

Date: _____

Today, I feel…

Today, I am so happy and grateful for:

1. _____

2. _____

3. _____

What is your favourite animal?

_____

Can you list 3 things that your favourite animal can do?

1. _____

2. _____

3. _____

> **Repeat 3 times:**
> **I am enough**

Find a Way

Let's help our little friend to reach his piggy-bank!
Don't forget to take the additional coin on the way!

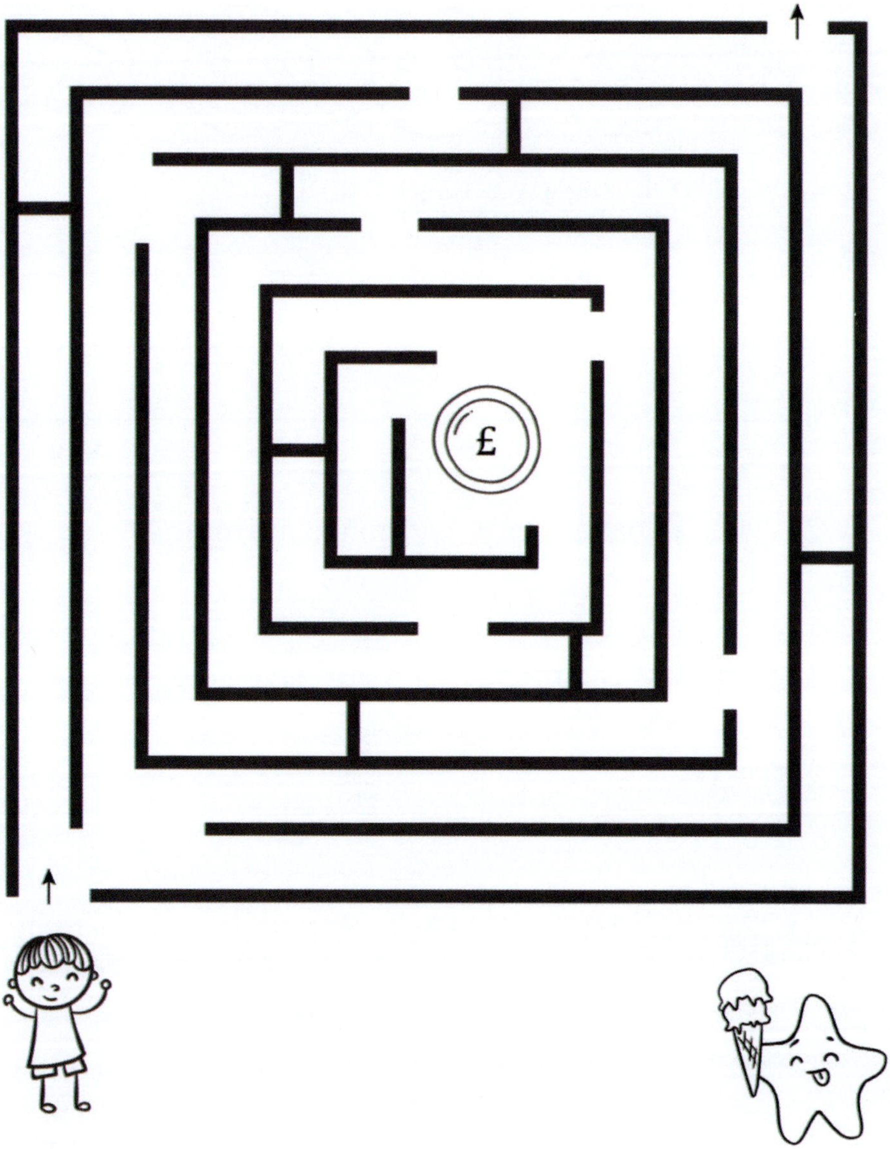

Day 3

Date: _____

Today, I feel…

Today, I am so happy and grateful for:

1. _____
2. _____
3. _____

What is your favourite colour?

_____

Can you name 3 things that are that colour?

1. _____
2. _____
3. _____

> **Repeat 3 times:**
> **I am amazing**

My Favourite People

Write all the words in the jar that come into your mind
to describe your **favourite people**
(e.g.: fun, kind)

Kind   Fun

Day 4

Date: _____

Today, I feel…

Today, I am so happy and grateful for:

1. _____
2. _____
3. _____

Where would you love to go on holiday?

_____

_____

Would you like to do when you are there?

_____

_____

> **Repeat 3 times:**
> **I forgive myself for my mistakes**

What Would You Choose?

Read the statements below. Which make you feel good? Colour them in. Think about why they make you feel good - is it because you would like someone to do that to or for you for example?

- Be kind to someone
- Snatch something of someone
- Shouting with a cross voice at someone
- Putting your toys away when you're finished with them.

Day 5

Date: _____

Today, I feel…

Today, I am so happy and grateful for:

1. _____

2. _____

3. _____

Write about something that happened today that you didn't like (e.g. I got into trouble for leaving by toys on the floor)	How would you have liked it to have happened? (e.g. I put my toys away when I was finished with them and everyone was happy)

Tick what you have done today:

- ○ Cleaned the table after a meal
- ○ Fed a pet
- ○ Picked up litter
- ○ Spoke nicely to someone today
- ○ Said please and thank you today
- ○ Wrote a nice note for someone
- ○ Played a sport today

Repeat 3 times:
I get better every single day

What is your favourite toy? Can you draw a picture of it?

Right Now...

Sit quietly and answer the statement below.

Right now, as I sit here, I can see...

_____

_____

_____

Can you draw a picture of one of those things?

Day 6

Date: _____

Today, I feel…

Today, I am so happy and grateful for:

1. _____

2. _____

3. _____

What two things would you like to do tomorrow? For example, finish reading my book and making extra effort in my chores tomorrow.

**Repeat 3 times:
I am brave**

If you were asked to design a new toy, what would you like to make? Draw a picture of it.

This or That

(Circle which would you choose out of these choices)

Tall	Small
Young	Old
Day	Night
TV	Cinema
Walk	Cycle
Summer	Winter
Cold	Hot
Fruit	Vegetables
Shorts	Trousers
Inside	Outside

Day 7

Date: _____

Today, I feel…

Today, I am so happy and grateful for:

1. _____
2. _____
3. _____

Where is your favourite place?

_____

_____

What do you like to do there?

_____

_____

**Repeat 3 times:
I am always learning**

Fun Activity

Take a Breath

- Sit down on a seat or on the floor
- Take a slow deep breath in through your nose
- Notice the feel of the air in your nose as you breathe in and feel your chest rise
- Then breathe out through your nose (or your mouth if you prefer)
- Notice your chest fall
- Repeat this 20 times slowly or for 1 minute

Day 8

Date: _____

Today, I feel…

Today, I am so happy and grateful for:

1. _____
2. _____
3. _____

What is your favourite thing to do in Winter?

_____

_____

Why do you like doing it?

_____

_____

**Repeat 3 times:
I am kind**

Colour the Picture!

Day 9

Date: _____

Today, I feel...

Today, I am so happy and grateful for:

1. _____

2. _____

3. _____

What two things would you like to do tomorrow? For example, finish reading my book and making extra effort in my chores tomorrow.

**Repeat 3 times:
I am caring**

What is your favourite animal?
Can you draw a picture of it?

What Would You Choose?

Read the statements below. Which make you feel good? Colour them in. Think about why they make you feel good - is it because you would like someone to do that to or for you for example?

Saying something nice to someone

Making a card for someone special

Not doing something you have been asked to do

Telling someone you don't like them

Day 10

Date: _____

Today, I feel…

Today, I am so happy and grateful for:

1. _____

2. _____

3. _____

Write about something that happened today that you didn't like	How would you have liked it to have happened?

Tick what you have done today:

○ Smiled at someone
○ Told someone I loved them
○ Learned to spell a new word
○ Talked about my feelings today
○ Spoke nicely to someone today
○ Say 3 things that I am good at to myself
○ Read a chapter of a book

| **Repeat 3 times:** **I am calm** | Design a new pair of socks. |

Right Now...

Sit quietly and answer the statement below.

Right now, as I sit here, I can hear...

_____

_____

_____

Can you draw a picture of one of those things?

Day 11

Date: _____

Today, I feel...

Today, I am so happy and grateful for:

1. _____
2. _____
3. _____

Name 1 thing you would like to learn more about.

_____

Can you find out 3 things about it that you do not already know?

_____
_____
_____

> **Repeat 3 times:**
> **I am loved**

Favourite Foods

Can you draw your favourite foods on this plate?

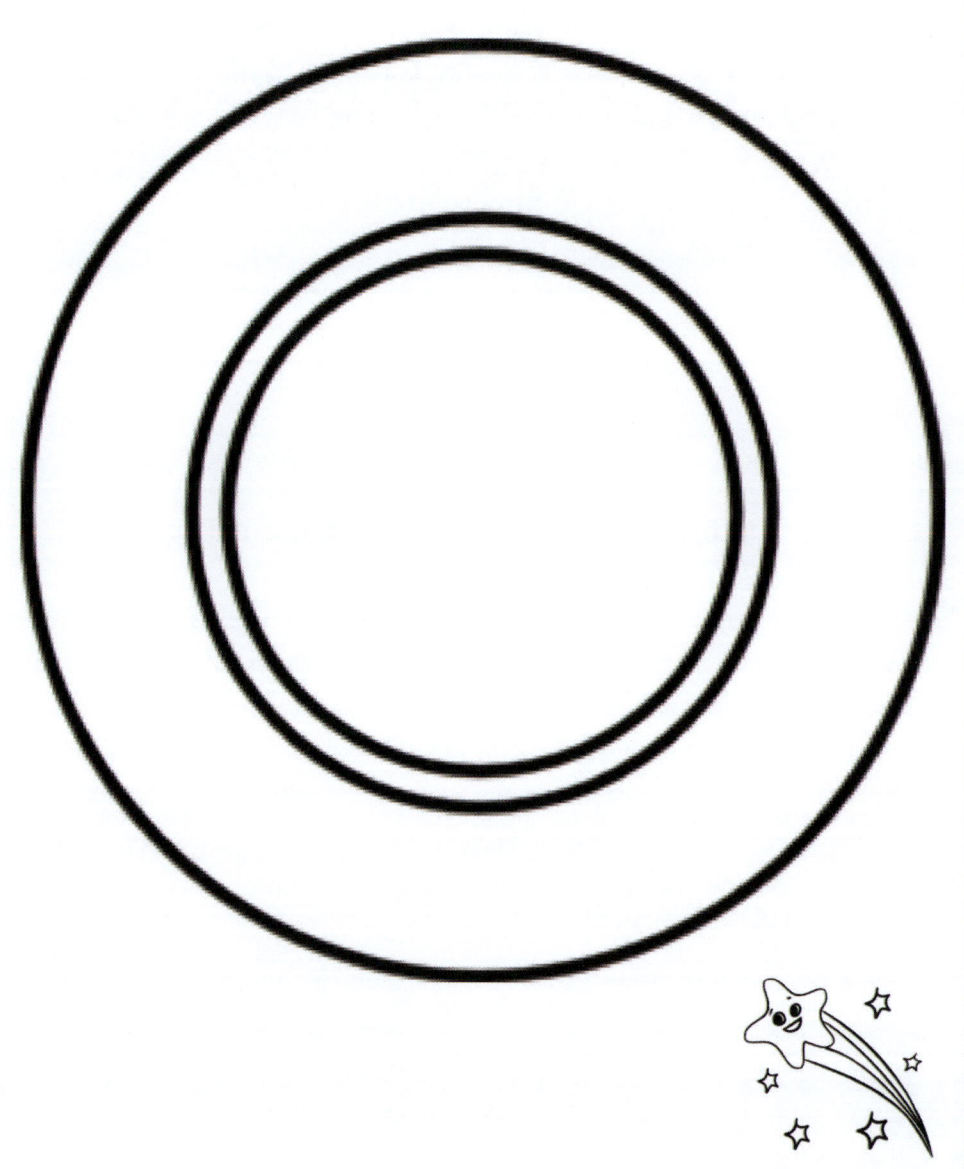

Day 12

Date: _____

Today, I feel…

Today, I am so happy and grateful for:

1. _____

2. _____

3. _____

What would you like to be when you grow up and why?

_____

_____

_____

_____

_____

**Repeat 3 times:
Learning is my super-power**

Favourite Foods

Write all the words in the jar that come into your mind to describe your favourite **foods**.
(e.g.: delicious)

Delicious

Day 13

Date: _____

Today, I feel…

Today, I am so happy and grateful for:

1. _____
2. _____
3. _____

Name 5 things that makes you happy!

_____
_____
_____
_____
_____

**Repeat 3 times:
I am grateful**

Colours

```
S D Y E O B R O W N C S N U I
Q B Q N Q R C D L J B S F U G
Q F Y L I T A M H V F L Y Q R
A Z P I N K R N G R J L A H E
P R E D Y L W W G R Q C Y C Y
O Y X F E N F H C E E R O E K
R A Q H L J P I X A Z E E U L
V D T D L K S T R J V H N S S
A C S E O B L E S L E A L Z D
X D I P W O S T D P V A M D N
D M L M S K M Z D R U E Q S O
Z L V I A Q R M D A B R C M C
C C E Y J G P Y M E L R P U L
S R R M A N J S S X U F T L R
M V Z W E Q O A C K E X X V E
```

Purple   Yellow   Orange   Silver
Green   Brown   Pink   Black
Red   White   Blue   Grey

Day 14

Date: _____

Today, I feel…

Today, I am so happy and grateful for:

1. _____

2. _____

3. _____

Tick what you have done today:

○ Brushed my teeth
○ Exercised today
○ Drank water today
○ Gave someone a hug
○ Cleaned the table after a meal
○ Picked up litter
○ Smiled at someone

Name 5 things that makes you happy.

_____

_____

_____

_____

_____

Repeat 3 times:
I am unique

Colour the Picture!

Day 15

Date: _____

Today, I feel…

Today, I am so happy and grateful for:

1. _____

2. _____

3. _____

What two things would you like to do tomorrow? For example, finish reading my book and making extra effort in my chores tomorrow.

Repeat 3 times: I love to try new things

Draw something that makes you happy.

Write the First Thing

What is the first thing you think of when you read these words:
For example:
Wet - water or pool or rain or bath

Red	
Green	
Black	
White	
Pink	
Blue	
Purple	
Orange	
Brown	
Yellow	

Day 16

Date: _____

Today, I feel...

Today, I am so happy and grateful for:

1. _____

2. _____

3. _____

Write about something that happened today that you didn't like	How would you have liked it to have happened?

| **Repeat 3 times: I am happy** | Design a t-shirt. |

Fun Activity

Make a Glitter Jar

- Find a clear jar or a plastic bottle with a lid
- Fill the jar or bottle up to ¾ full with water (you can add food colouring if you want)
- Add clear glue and glitter
- Seal the lid
- Shake

Day 17

Date: _____

Today, I feel…

Today, I am so happy and grateful for:

1. _____
2. _____
3. _____

What was the best thing that happened today and why was it so good?

_____
_____
_____
_____
_____

**Repeat 3 times:
I am creative**

Colour the Picture!

Who am I?
I am a _____.

Day 18

Date: _____

Today, I feel…

Today, I am so happy and grateful for:

1. _____

2. _____

3. _____

Tick what you have done today:
- ○ Fed a pet
- ○ Helped someone at home
- ○ Made my bed
- ○ Talked about my feelings
- ○ Learned something new
- ○ Cleaned the table after a meal
- ○ Played a sport today

What would you like to eat on a picnic?

_____

_____

_____

_____

_____

> **Repeat 3 times:**
> **I am clever**

What Would You Choose?

Read the statements below. Which make you feel good? Colour them in. Think about why they make you feel good - is it because you would like someone to do that to or for you for example?

- Helping someone do something
- Dropping litter on the ground
- Throwing a toy and hitting someone with it
- Smiling

Day 19

Date: _____

Today, I feel…

Today, I am so happy and grateful for:

1. _____

2. _____

3. _____

Draw a picture of someone that you love.

**Repeat 3 times:
I am wise**

This or That

(Circle which would you choose out of these choices)

Beach	Country
Chocolate	Fruit
Water	Snow
Swing	Slide
Go Kart	Motorbike
Read	Watch
Trainers	Shoes
Slippers	Socks
Phone	Computer
Hot Chocolate	Smoothie

Day 20

Date: _____

Today, I feel…

Today, I am so happy and grateful for:

1. _____

2. _____

3. _____

What two things would you like to do tomorrow? For example, finish reading my book and making extra effort in my chores tomorrow.

**Repeat 3 times:
I am honest**

If you could be a character in a book, what would your name be? Can you draw a picture of you as this character?

Months

```
G S G K Q J X K U Q J N N M Q
N L F C I A C V G Y U T U A R
V E E Y Y N A P R I L C A R W
R P B J M U I Q H M Y E U C G
W B R G I A T R B C O F G H R
Z O U K S R B N W K I F U D O
S Y A H I Y Y Z O N P C S E V
E T R Y C N W E C V W I T C O
M L Y B G C Z P K B E G J E R
G A G O O C T O B E R M S M Y
Y N Y O E W J W M B J G B B O
C M Q U C D S Q S R U W N E R
N X Z S C N Q P W W N E H R R
U L U K J Q A I S D E R R L H
G S E P T E M B E R N I G B S
```

September   February   November   December
January   August   October   March
April   June   May   July

Day 21

Date: _____

Today, I feel…

Today, I am so happy and grateful for:

1. _____

2. _____

3. _____

Write about something that happened today that you didn't like	How would you have liked it to have happened?

Tick what you have done today:

○ Offer help to a family member or friend
○ Learned the meaning of a new word/phrase
○ Exercised today
○ Wrote a nice note for someone
○ Said please and thank you today
○ Told someone 3 things I liked about them
○ Did a chore without being asked

Repeat 3 times:
I am fun

What is your favourite treat to eat? Can you draw it?

Right Now...

Sit quietly and answer the statement below.

Right now, as I sit here, I can touch...

_____

_____

_____

Can you draw a picture of one of those things?

Day 22

Date: _____

Today, I feel…

Today, I am so happy and grateful for:

1. _____
2. _____
3. _____

Can you design a hat?

**Repeat 3 times:
I am thankful**

Colour the Picture!

Who am I?
I am a _____.

Day 23

Date: _____

Today, I feel…

Today, I am so happy and grateful for:

1. _____
2. _____
3. _____

If you were going on a trip and were only allowed to take 3 things, what would they be and why?

_____
_____
_____
_____
_____

> **Repeat 3 times:**
> **I enjoy learning**

Day 24

Date: _____

Today, I feel…

Today, I am so happy and grateful for:

1. _____

2. _____

3. _____

Tick what you have done today:

○ Picked up litter
○ Smiled at someone
○ Gave someone a hug
○ Learned to spell a new word
○ Drank water today
○ Fed a pet
○ Brushed my teeth

What 3 things do you like to do at the park?

_____
_____
_____
_____
_____

**Repeat 3 times:
I am a great friend**

Your Super-Hero Powers

If you were a Super-Hero, what would your special powers be?
Write them below and describe how you would use
them to do good things.

Day 25

Date: _____

Today, I feel…

Today, I am so happy and grateful for:

1. _____

2. _____

3. _____

What two things would you like to do tomorrow? For example, finish reading my book and making extra effort in my chores tomorrow.

**Repeat 3 times:
I am awesome**

What 3 toppings would you put on a pizza?
Can you draw it?

My Feelings Jar

Write all the words in the jar that come into your mind to describe your **feelings**
(e.g.: happy)

Happy

Day 26

Date: _____

Today, I feel…

Today, I am so happy and grateful for:

1. _____

2. _____

3. _____

What is your most favourite thing to do in Summer?

_____

_____

Why do you like to do it and who do you like to do it with?

_____

_____

**Repeat 3 times:
I am confident**

Sports

```
C V J N E T B A L L A M W X H X U R N F
I N C U W A L K I N G I G H P N Z A G Q
X A K H H R O U W J N N K O Y Y X G F X
G M C B D B L L C G A X Y E M W C V C C
C O E X C D A W R Y Y D A X P H H K Y R
U H L V P A S R Z L C M S P W T I I O A
W P M F U N N F X W S L N I N P K F G L
A X W Y Y Q L O C U Y O I A C D I M A L
S W I M M I N G E D B K B N S D N H M Y
X S R A C O F M E I A J Y F G T G I D I
A S U Y V T N O Q D N K O D O M I U Y N
B T I C E B M U O X G G U C F U A C T G
S I G X B A S K E T B A L L M I V U S F
E Z F I I A X N R F B E T I Z F Y D G B
I Y E G Z B J K U W O A W D O I E U P X
L S S D A N C E N I A H L D P D U Z A B
I R Y X F U K J I O X F A L X I O R Q A
N V C N Z Y F J R O E B O X P Y Z O O P
G K C F B D G X C L I M B I N G N B Z A
D E H P E Z E K E W W M N M O F E L H O
```

Basketball	Gymnastics	Abseiling	Football	Golf
Climbing	Swimming	Rallying	Canoeing	Yoga
Walking	Cycling	Netball	Dance	Hiking

Day 27

Date: _____

Today, I feel…

Today, I am so happy and grateful for:

1. _____

2. _____

3. _____

Write about something that happened today that you didn't like	How would you have liked it to have happened?

Tick what you have done today:
- ○ Told someone I loved them
- ○ Cleaned the table after a meal
- ○ Say 3 things that I am good at to myself
- ○ Talked about my feelings today
- ○ Drew a nice picture for someone
- ○ Spoke nicely to someone today
- ○ Learned the meaning of a new word/phrase

Repeat 3 times:
I am strong

Draw something that makes you laugh.

Colour the Picture!

Who am I?
I am a _____.

Day 28

Date: _____

Today, I feel…

Today, I am so happy and grateful for:

1. _____
2. _____
3. _____

Can you tell me 3 things you can use water for?

_____

_____

_____

_____

_____

**Repeat 3 times:
I am smart**

This or That

(Circle which would you choose out of these choices)

Quiet	Loud
Strawberry	Orange
Shells	Rocks
Straight	Round
Fly	Drive
Swim	Run
Popcorn	Crisps
Lie Down	Stand Up
Shower	Bath
Draw	Paint

Day 29

Date: _____

Today, I feel…

Today, I am so happy and grateful for:

1. _____

2. _____

3. _____

What is the best thing about your school? Can you draw a picture of it?

**Repeat 3 times:
I always try my best**

What Would You Choose?

Read the statements below. Which make you feel good? Colour them in. Think about why they make you feel good - is it because you would like someone to do that to or for you for example?

- Dancing to music
- Having fun with your best friend
- Hurting someone
- Taking something that you're not allowed to

Day 30

Date: _____

Today, I feel...

Today, I am so happy and grateful for:

1. _____

2. _____

3. _____

What two things would you like to do tomorrow? For example, finish reading my book and making extra effort in my chores tomorrow.

Repeat 3 times: I am a great listener

What is your favourite drink? Can you draw it?

Types of Clothes

```
G Y M Y L D X J P V X V R I Z C Z A E Q
Q T W U W L V E O Q J B Z F Q P O O X U
K G I U M F D P F N N G J I V D D A J D
S D R E S S P H V G I S J U M P E R T E
H K E S C R O E M P F Z C M H X V I K X
I P X U B L O U S E S A M A H P O Y P H
R O T Z L O T A C C Y B A A R G W A C E
T D K O W G Z D Z D G F H M S F Q R Z I
S C R A S X Q D A A Y D Y J P Q Z U L H
A V U V T X P X L G E J O B U G X D Y B
Z L D I J S L Y P X V K K P S S D X R N
K B C Y X Z L I J C O W B A S T P V J Q
I E S C I N I H U A J E A N S Y N X V G
S K I R T L S R G O M E S O C K S D Z T
Y D T L B K H U R A I A C V A Q I X A U
N E S K X E O S B A E J S R O O N H H L
A G U B K H R T G E C C V H V O H T G T
V D I C H B T D D O C R G Q U E V Z O K
K E T Z B O S G V P E A F K V Y S A O H
K M F T R O U S E R S G P A N T S T I B
```

Trousers	Pyjamas	Jumper	Shorts	Shirts
Blouse	Scarf	Skirt	Jeans	Pants
Socks	Dress	Coat	Vest	Suit

Day 31

Date: _____

Today, I feel…

Today, I am so happy and grateful for:

1. _____

2. _____

3. _____

Write about something that happened today that you didn't like	How would you have liked it to have happened?

Tick what you have done today:

- ○ Played a sport today
- ○ Made my bed
- ○ Smiled at someone
- ○ Gave someone a hug
- ○ Said please and thank you today
- ○ Say good morning & good night to my family
- ○ Read a chapter of a book

Repeat 3 times:
I love challenges

Draw something that makes you smile.

Colour the Picture!

Who am I?
I am a _____.

Day 32

Date: _____

Today, I feel…

Today, I am so happy and grateful for:

1. _____

2. _____

3. _____

What is your favourite song?

_____

How does it make you feel when you hear it?

_____

_____

_____

_____

> **Repeat 3 times:**
> **I always tell the truth**

Favourite Games

Write all the words in the jar that come into your mind to describe your **favourite games.**
(e.g.: fun)

Fun

Day 33

Date: _____

Today, I feel…

Today, I am so happy and grateful for:

1. _____
2. _____
3. _____

What do you like to daydream about?

_____
_____
_____
_____
_____

**Repeat 3 times:
I am successful**

Fun Activity

Go for a Mindful Walk

- Go outside with an adult
- Go for a walk
- Remember you need to stay quiet so that you can:
    - Notice all the sounds that there are - birds, animals, cars, alarms, wind, water
    - Notice any smells
    - Notice any flowers, trees, buildings animals, clouds, etc
- Enjoy

Day 34

Date: _____

Today, I feel...

Today, I am so happy and grateful for:

1. _____
2. _____
3. _____

Tick what you have done today:

○ Spoke nicely to someone today
○ Picked up litter
○ Helped someone at home
○ Cleaned the table after a meal
○ Told someone I loved them
○ Exercised today
○ Talked about my feelings today

Where is your favourite place to relax and why?

_____
_____
_____
_____
_____

**Repeat 3 times:
I believe in myself**

Family Members

```
T P B X U S N I W I Q B X T T Q D K R B
M H S J U B A B R O T H E R C O O Z C X
Q D A D N Q D U W P L X I D S N A J E U
W P D B L P G N N O Y C J D D W A Z G O
D D G C C U W R G T G R A N D C H I L D
R A I J J Q N T A R I I V B N I W N I N
Q D D M O T B C D N X E S J X J N C L I
H D H R F C Q M L H N J O A Q D G P Z R
Q Y Y Y K D J E D E I Y N Q V F B E R K
J J C W P Y I W A K Q U S E T O R U R D
V N D W E H D I N L B C O U S I N U I N
I Q B G R A N D A E K T U R B K X M E A
O H M X N E I C E D P W E J R H B U J U
T E Y H M J C S R P V H D P S A U Q V Q
Q O H H I N G Z P E C C E N O I U R E V
D A U G H T E R A B I Z M W G E S K A V
V B L F S U W G Z F D W U R S Q X T H N
Y P N O Q X U J D I T W M K T Q J Z E E
O L E Q I H K U C K D N M V R A J E A R
U D P X L V M S Q I O D Y N J X M U S N
```

Grandchild	Daughter	Brother	Granny
Granda	Sister	Auntie	Nephew
Cousin	Mummy	Daddy	Uncle
	Neice	Son	

Day 35

Date: _____

Today, I feel…

Today, I am so happy and grateful for:

1. _____

2. _____

3. _____

> What two things would you like to do tomorrow? For example, finish reading my book and making extra effort in my chores tomorrow.

What are 3 things you like about your best friend?

_____

_____

_____

> **Repeat 3 times:**
> **I am perfect the way I am**

Write the First Thing

What is the first thing you think of when you read these words:
For example:
Wet - water or pool or rain or bath

Brave	
Surprise	
Calm	
Sad	
Cheerful	
Tearful	
Excited	
Love	
Shocked	
Hope	

Day 36

Date: _____

Today, I feel…

Today, I am so happy and grateful for:

1. _____

2. _____

3. _____

Write about something that happened today that you didn't like	How would you have liked it to have happened?

What 3 things would you like to change about your school?

_____

_____

_____

Repeat 3 times:
I work hard

Colour the Picture!

Who am I?
I am a _____.

Day 37

Date: _____

Today, I feel…

Today, I am so happy and grateful for:

1. _____
2. _____
3. _____

Name 3 people who makes you smile and explain why do they make you smile?

_____
_____
_____
_____
_____

**Repeat 3 times:
I am love**

Right Now...

Sit quietly and answer the statement below.

Right now, as I sit here, I can smell...

_____

_____

_____

Can you draw a picture of one of those things?

Day 38

Date: _____

Today, I feel...

Today, I am so happy and grateful for:

1. _____
2. _____
3. _____

Design a jumper.

**Repeat 3 times:
I am forgiving**

Countries

```
I A M F R T C S S B R V E Z K N W H F A
X U A J Q P D C J R U H X V X F A P L R
C S G Q W O S V L N S F R A N C E U S V
H T V C X L S F X C S Q E K W X D D U J
I R K I R A U G W K I M W N X X F A K I
N A L V W N M G Q R A E W L B C W O V N
A L I K T D V S G Z O Q B R A Z I L S M
I I D A W P I S T L D F T L D X I H P W
B A Z H V Y I T I V N B W A H B S R I Z
L V L J S M W Q A O R K K B I I P R R A
C R Y F D N H I P L A G S O I N A T E V
J A O G E R M A N Y Y Y A V Q V I P L M
S T N W W L U W W D I P A A M F N V A F
L H G A I Y O Z G J I K U F M P J P N Q
F Y K Y D B A F R I C A M N F E D H D V
Q O Q M K A K T A M C X B S H P R L V R
P Y Q M Y R E W M R Z G Y Q Q F O I A I
Z P R C O O L T U K U W I L Q G N K C T
R H B X N D U U R T H Z S M K I L A G A
B E N G L A N D M E X I C O Z Z Y H S U
```

Australia	America	England	Ireland
Germany	Russia	Canada	Brazil
Mexico	France	Africa	Poland
China	India	Italy	Spain

Day 39

Date: _____

Today, I feel…

Today, I am so happy and grateful for:

1. _____

2. _____

3. _____

Tick what you have done today:
- ○ Made my bed
- ○ Brushed my teeth
- ○ Learned to spell a new word
- ○ Fed a pet
- ○ Gave someone a hug
- ○ Drank water today
- ○ Helped someone at home

What do you like most about your family?

_____

_____

_____

_____

_____

> **Repeat 3 times:**
> **I am beautiful inside and out**

Fun Activity

Heart Rate Changes

- Sit on a seat and place your hand over your heart.
- Can you feel your heart beat? Is it fast? Is it strong?
- Stand up.
- Can you do 1 of these exercises for 1 minute?
  - Running on the spot
  - Jump up and down
  - Run around your garden
- Sit down again and place your hand over your heart
- Can you feel your heart beat now? Is it faster? Is it stronger?
- How long does it take to go back to normal?

Day 40

Date: _____

Today, I feel...

Today, I am so happy and grateful for:

1. _____

2. _____

3. _____

What two things would you like to do tomorrow? For example, finish reading my book and making extra effort in my chores tomorrow.

Who is the kindest person you know and what makes them kind?

_____

_____

_____

> **Repeat 3 times:**
> **I choose my own attitude**

Colour the Picture!

Day 41

Date: _____

Today, I feel…

Today, I am so happy and grateful for:

1. _____
2. _____
3. _____

What is your favourite thing to do in Autumn?

_____

Why do you like doing it?

_____

_____

_____

_____

Repeat 3 times:
I care for others

My Hobbies

Write all the words in the jar that come into your mind to describe your **hobbies.**
(e.g.: drawing)

Drawing

Day 42

Date: _____

Today, I feel…

Today, I am so happy and grateful for:

1. _____
2. _____
3. _____

Draw something that you think is fun to do.

**Repeat 3 times:
I am helpful**

Food

```
H Y D G R S A T A S V I Z P P N T S J U
E F H X A A T T P D O J B P O T M Z X J
W E R C U X X W C A U N A V N G T D S R
P N W O N F Y N R W S Y F Z I I U N U E
M D S Z R N B S X J O T Z R O S R E U G
A L N T K U R Z L E R M A X N A K O B K
J P O T A T O O H Y G L X A U A E S I C
H V C D S O C P I K Y I P W S L Y U A J
G X H B R X C E Y C G U M V X Q V C C F
F B E T A M O P B C N U L Y M H W A L P
P L E F O A L P R H Y D U N B F C R V G
E L S P H M I E E I F M S D D O F R K U
A F E D X F A R A C Y E P Z Y N F O J T
S D K V O Z M T D K E A F N P W W T W N
K L E T T U C E O E S T O Z W S N S D X
Z Y C P X W B X N N S F M O B L F L P H
X A O X A Z A E X V J D I I T P U F W I
X K S Z R B Z D X E Q T G C D M T U D S
H N D G L L B A P P I J P J V O Y S H X
K O Q P A T C W C H I P S A U S A G E R
```

Broccoli   Chicken   Sausage   Lettuce
Carrots   Cheese   Pepper   Tomato
Potato   Turkey   Bread   Chips
Pasta   Onion   Meat   Peas

Day 43

Date: _____

Today, I feel…

Today, I am so happy and grateful for:

1. _____

2. _____

3. _____

Write about something that happened today that you didn't like	How would you have liked it to have happened?

If you had 3 wishes, what would they be?

_____

_____

_____

Repeat 3 times:
I love my life

Fun Activity

Time to Relax Your Body

Take your time to squeeze each part of body/muscle for 5 seconds and then release it again.
- Crunch up your toes really tight and count to 5 and then release them again
- Next make your legs really straight so that no one can move them for 5 seconds
- Squeeze your bum really tight for 5 seconds
- Make your tummy hard like you would if someone smaller sits on it for 5 seconds
- Squeeze your chest tight for 5 seconds
- Make your arms really straight so that no one can move them for 5 seconds
- Squeeze your fingers into a tight fist - pretend you have a secret inside your fist that you won't let anyone get for 5 seconds
- Lift your shoulders up to your ears and count to 5 then drop them away again
- Bite your teeth really hard for 5 seconds
- Open your mouth really wide for 5 seconds
- Scrunch up your nose for 5 seconds
- Squeeze your eyes tight for 5 seconds
- Lift your eyebrows really high for 5 seconds
- Notice how your body feels now - it is nice and relaxed

Day 44

Date: _____

Today, I feel…

Today, I am so happy and grateful for:

1. _____
2. _____
3. _____

What is your favourite thing to do at the weekend?
_____

Why do you like doing it?
_____
_____
_____
_____

**Repeat 3 times:
I am healthy**

Colour the Picture!

Day 45

Date: _____

Today, I feel…

Today, I am so happy and grateful for:

1. _____
2. _____
3. _____

What two things would you like to do tomorrow? For example, finish reading my book and making extra effort in my chores tomorrow.

Can you name your 3 favourite movies?

_____
_____
_____

**Repeat 3 times:
I am friendly**

Find a Way

It's time for a holiday! Can you find the right car with the right destination to the beach?

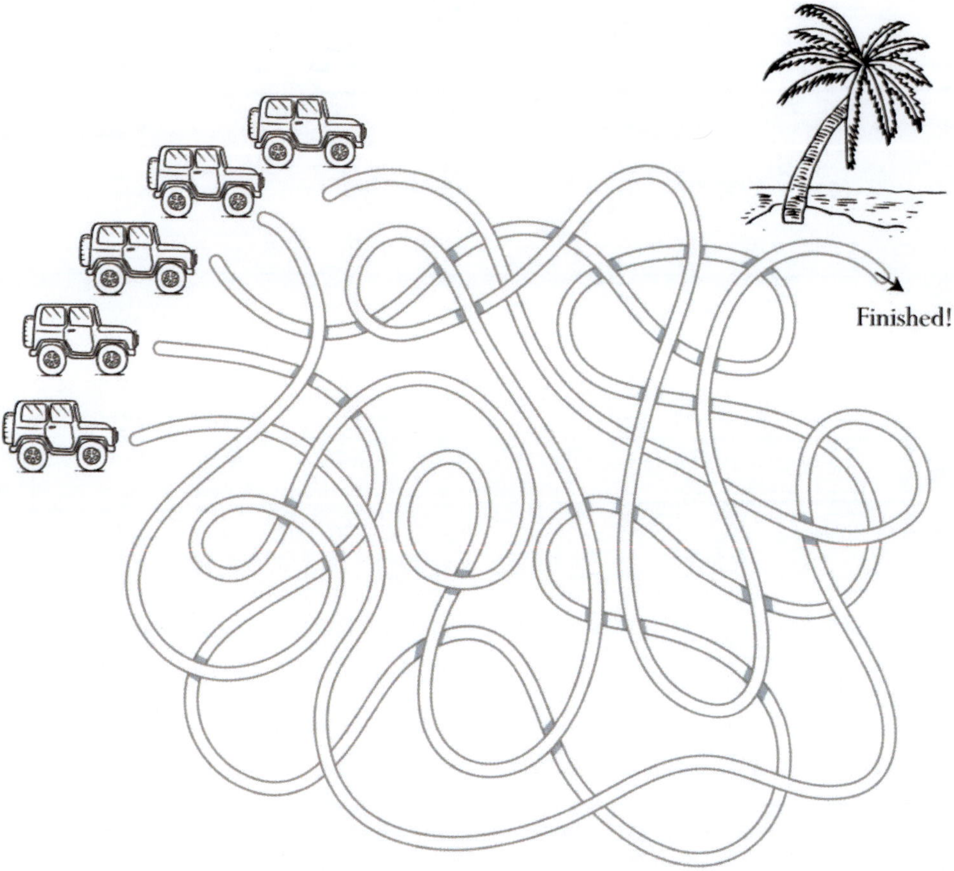

Finished!

Day 46

Date: _____

Today, I feel...

Today, I am so happy and grateful for:

1. _____
2. _____
3. _____

Tick what you have done today:

- ○ Cleaned the table after a meal
- ○ Learned something new today
- ○ Offer help to a family or friend
- ○ Wrote a nice note for someone
- ○ Spoke nicely to someone today
- ○ Did a chore without being asked
- ○ Told someone 3 things I liked about them

Who makes you feel loved and why?

_____
_____
_____
_____
_____

**Repeat 3 times:
I am worthy**

Fruit

```
M G Z M Y H C N A W B L U E B E R R Y P
C Y T W L A D V E N L G A P X Q X G C N
D Z X T L V P K Y C R X O P U G V H S P
P G R X H H W P C C T M D S S M I C C E
E R B D F O I P L Q T A A I P I Z J D A
A A N L Y R Q L Z E F X R G Q Z Q N I R
C P T L A X P U I A W L G I F U Q T S T
H E S I W C F M P A S S I O N F R U I T
H S T M E N K M K L Z P V I S E T N M P
M J R E Y P C B R Y R Y U G W Q K A B G
O N A P A I I D E I B U O R A N G E X J
X H W Y R B T N C R Q A W R W X C X R A
R I B U D A R I E D R M N G Q K A V H Y
H R E I L T S O H A N Y G A D A F D U O
K L R Q Q X V P B V P N Q F N V M F I L
E O R W U A O I B Y Z P K R O A Q P O B
A C Y S T O G I M E S H L E T M K E Z N
N W N U S K H E O K R X Y E T L E M O N
D X U G U M J E G S T R F W T I K Z E C
D O A V G H B Y G Y W Y Y K H N A A U B
```

Passionfruit   Blackberry   Pineapple   Strawberry
Raspberry   Orange   Nectarine   Banana
Grapes   Apple   Peach   Blueberry
Lemon   Plum   Lime   Pear

Day 47

Date: _____

Today, I feel…

Today, I am so happy and grateful for:

1. _____

2. _____

3. _____

If you were asked to do something nice for someone in your family today, what would you do and who would you do it for?

_____

_____

_____

_____

Repeat 3 times:
I am capable

Colour the Picture!

Day 48

Date: _____

Today, I feel…

Today, I am so happy and grateful for:

1. _____

2. _____

3. _____

Write about something that happened today that you didn't like	How would you have liked it to have happened?

What 3 things do you like to do at the beach?

_____

_____

_____

Repeat 3 times:
I am proud of myself

What Would You Choose?

Read the statements below. Which make you feel good? Colour them in. Think about why they make you feel good - is it because you would like someone to do that to or for you for example?

- Singing your favourite song
- Staying quiet while someone else is speaking
- Crossing the road without looking
- Leaving your shoes in the middle of the floor

Day 49

Date: _____

Today, I feel…

Today, I am so happy and grateful for:

1. _____
2. _____
3. _____

Who do you like to spend a lot of time with?

_____

What do you like to do with them most?

_____

_____

_____

**Repeat 3 times:
I love to be silent**

Colour the Picture!

Day 50

Date: _____

Today, I feel...

Today, I am so happy and grateful for:

1. _____

2. _____

3. _____

What two things would you like to do tomorrow? For example, finish reading my book and making extra effort in my chores tomorrow.

Where is your favourite place to play and why?

_____

_____

_____

> **Repeat 3 times:**
> **I choose to think positively**

Christmas

```
Z O A Z J H N T K L F X F D B A X W M U
B T I C N N D A R U I Q M M C W P Y B W
K M G D V O D H B U Q E R P Z G B G V A
G A J G X I Y T U X H Z X Q X J A G F V
U N P W A C N S A N T A N R N A O D O I
M G W Y C T V Q K D K K N L S Y F Y I F
P E R E I N D E E R M S V C A N D L E S
M L B R A M I N C E P I E X C D O U P Z
I I H M C C I Z O D T J E P K E S H M W
W N L M Y C U P C X W S N Q W X T J D J
L Q L K Z D V U Q B G H D T O T O T A L
M U M Q R B O U W J D A D P X R C I G P
S O C G Z A V K X L X Y R M D E K N G Y
D E Q U R U Q L M J O S W L A E I S C W
Q X B K D B C P R Z E T M Q A Y N E U I
Y V V Y A Z L R S T A R O A I S N G L M T
L S A M J E J H A E V A P K N P D Y L B
E L T D Y S E H R G X E D L O N T K V I
I P R E S E N T S C J Y R Q W J G O F C
F V L Y C V C A R R O T V W O R N M S U
```

Stocking	Reindeer	Mince Pie	Presents
Garland	Baubles	Tinsel	Candle
Angel	Santa	Tree	Carrot
Star	Milk	Sack	Snow

Day 51

Date: _____

Today, I feel...

Today, I am so happy and grateful for:

1. _____
2. _____
3. _____

What is your favourite thing to do in Spring?
_____

Why do you like doing it?
_____
_____
_____

> **Repeat 3 times:**
> **I can talk about my feelings easily**

Right Now...

Sit quietly and answer the statement below.

Right now, as I sit here, I feel...

_____
_____
_____

Can you draw a picture of one of those things?

Day 52

Date: _____

Today, I feel…

Today, I am so happy and grateful for:

1. _____
2. _____
3. _____

Tick what you have done today:
- ○ Made my bed
- ○ Picked up litter
- ○ Drew a nice picture for someone
- ○ Smiled at someone
- ○ Brushed my teeth
- ○ Played a sport today
- ○ Say good morning and good night to my family

Can you name your 3 favourite songs?

_____
_____
_____
_____
_____

> **Repeat 3 times:**
> **I make good choices**

Colour the Picture!

Day 53

Date: _____

Today, I feel…

Today, I am so happy and grateful for:

1. _____
2. _____
3. _____

If you were asked to do something nice for someone in school today what would you do and who would you do it for?

_____
_____
_____

**Repeat 3 times:
I love to be active**

Pets

```
Q F M S S W M L D Y P K L W D O A B N S
N S O T V I R T R A B B I T O Z B P G Q
Y N X O C F W V O Q A M T L G P L K L H
L C O F D H J J R R K E U E J Q Q O Z P
N M O M J M X L R B T B L S I T U Y D G
K W B L B Q H X H U F O X H O V Z J P I
M W A M L Q B D B W K X I W E O Y K A V
U H D T B A Z C X M M J O S W X Y B R Y
P A X L E Z R O E T T T P R E Y H E R X
L M M Y R R Y V M V Q I P Q V L C S O P
T S E C A Z H E E A R N P M R X N X T J
H T L I Z A R D H B S P D F Y A K C V H
E E L U P Z R F W B Y I Y I Y E N L C Y
S R M I M K W I T C F M M S C X S I A F
F H X E L Z L L V K M T G H C E X C T B
M W L H Q R G X T K D R W N Q R O W R T
Q O H E S C B I R D Z E I H R C W S G P
Z R U N A W E A W B E A U Z Q I D Y D L
L C K S D D N H K V D T D S F S F S F D
V S O N E P M C I F E S C O O E O X T O
```

Tortoise	Exercise	Hamster	Rabbit
Parrot	Lizard	Collar	Treats
Mouse	Fish	Bird	Water
Food	Lead	Dog	Cat

Day 54

Date: _____

Today, I feel…

Today, I am so happy and grateful for:

1. _____

2. _____

3. _____

Write about something that happened today that you didn't like	How would you have liked it to have happened?

What 3 things makes someone a good friend?

_____

_____

_____

**Repeat 3 times:
Today is a great day**

Colour the Picture!

Day 55

Date: _____

Today, I feel...

Today, I am so happy and grateful for:

1. _____

2. _____

3. _____

What two things would you like to do tomorrow? For example, finish reading my book and making extra effort in my chores tomorrow.

What is your favourite thing to do at home?

_____

_____

_____

| **Repeat 3 times:** |
| **I am responsible** |

Colour the Picture!

Day 56

Date: _____

Today, I feel…

Today, I am so happy and grateful for:

1. _____

2. _____

3. _____

If you were able to, what famous person would you like to meet and why?

_____

_____

_____

_____

**Repeat 3 times:
I am generous**

My Wishes

Write all your **wishes** in the jar.
(I wish for…)

Day 57

Date: _____

Today, I feel...

Today, I am so happy and grateful for:

1. _____
2. _____
3. _____

Tick what you have done today:

- ○ Told someone I loved them
- ○ Fed a pet
- ○ Wrote a nice note for someone
- ○ Cleaned the table after a meal
- ○ Said please and thank you today
- ○ Drank water today
- ○ Say 3 things that I am good at to myself

Can you write the alphabet backwards, starting at Z?

_____
_____
_____
_____
_____

**Repeat 3 times:
I am full of life**

Farm Animals

```
J N A K K K U R A O G C U F J W R Q V G
C D J Q F D G K M C L T W S U X F V X L
A O S Q E E C A W D V G H C U B G P E P
T G Q N H U K U X U N W I O A K O I M O
L N R U B R H X U R L A M B R O A C G K
Q J I T S D D U L Z Q J N A P S T Y W P
P U S B J K I U N K B H M B P D E F S R
Y T W T K J L P C S Z G J Y V F B G P A
H N M Y N C C F T K O Q C U V T X R O L
L N S K H Z R Q F L T C H I C K E N X R
B X A R P W V O Z F A C A L F E H P C E
D S X O I L I F H M P I T J A Z M B W U
L Z J S G E Z U T M I P T G M I F H H L
S H B T D O Y X S T R S P V L F U H B Y
U V V E Q J D J D L Y R C B R M M W B C
B K I R Y B A L E W P C I U S B P E T P
R P S H E E P X U H K M L L G O O S E N
S T V C J H N P B I B D N L M B Z R T X
K X Y N M E H L L G I D G U G J Q C H D
U I C O W N B I L G R T V R W Q V H E N
```

Chicken	Roster	Horse	Sheep
Bull	Goose	Goat	Duck
Lamb	Calf	Cow	Cat
Dog	Hen	Pig	Hen

Day 58

Date: _____

Today, I feel…

Today, I am so happy and grateful for:

1. _____
2. _____
3. _____

What is your favourite thing to do outside?

_____
_____
_____
_____

Repeat 3 times:
I am able

Colour the Picture!

Day 59

Date: _____

Today, I feel...

Today, I am so happy and grateful for:

1. _____

2. _____

3. _____

Write about something that happened today that you didn't like	How would you have liked it to have happened?

Can you tell me 3 things you can make with wood?

_____

_____

_____

**Repeat 3 times:
I am bright**

Colour the Picture!

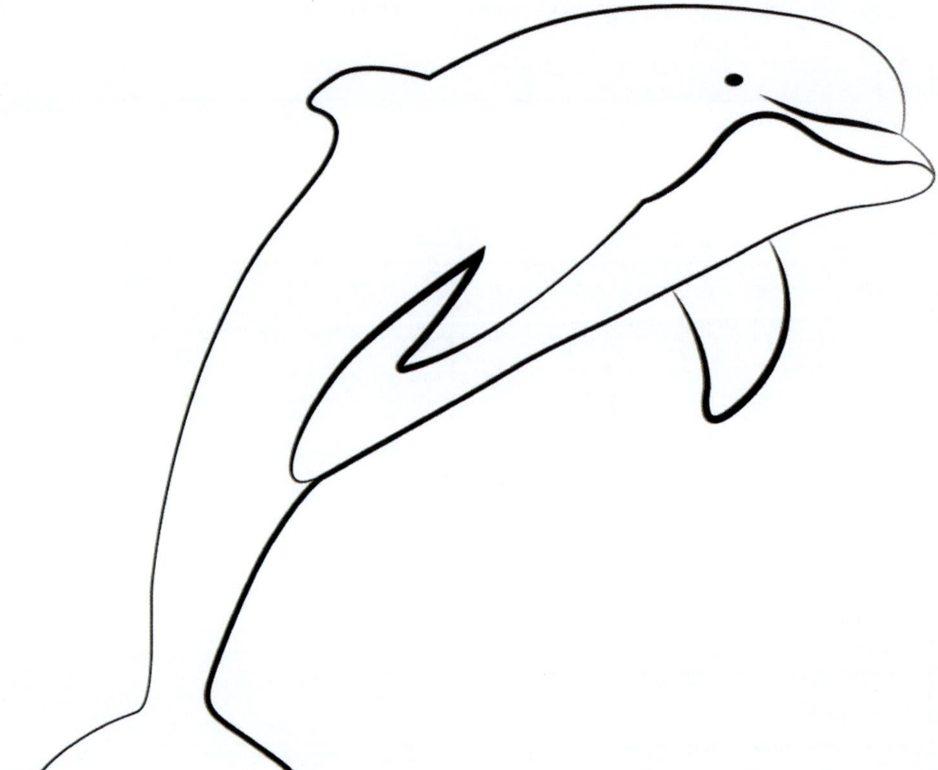

Day 60

Date: _____

Today, I feel…

Today, I am so happy and grateful for:

1. _____

2. _____

3. _____

What two things would you like to do tomorrow? For example, finish reading my book and making extra effort in my chores tomorrow.

Can you name your 3 favourite games?

_____

_____

_____

**Repeat 3 times:
I love to listen to others**

Answers

Who Am I

Day 18's Activity: Chemist

Day 23's Activity: Policeman

Day 28's Activity: Doctor

Day 32's Activity: Officeman

Day 37's Activity: Chef

Printed in Great Britain
by Amazon